POEMS

FROM THE

TABLE

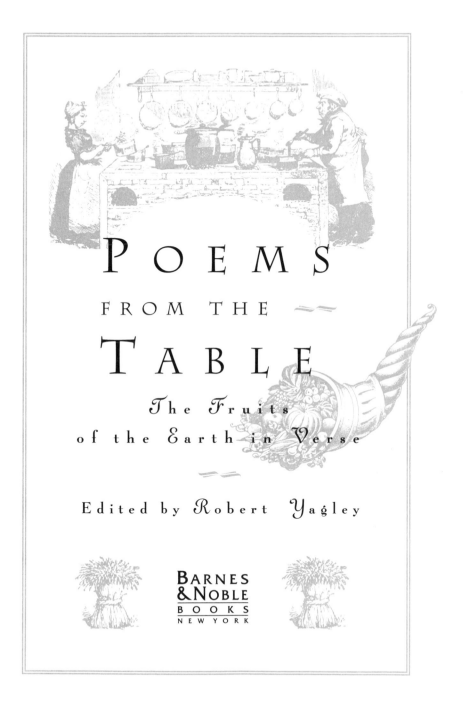

POEMS

FROM THE

TABLE

The Fruits
of the Earth in Verse

Edited by Robert Yagley

BARNES
&NOBLE
BOOKS
NEW YORK

This edition published by Barnes & Noble, Inc.

1995 Barnes & Noble Books

ISBN 1-56619-761-9

Printed and bound in the United States of America

2 4 6 8 10 M 9 7 5 3 1

$\mathcal{A}$cknowledgments

The editor would like to thank the poets, the poets' estates, and publishers involved for their prompt and cordial response to the permission requests to reprint the poems listed below. Also deserving a special thanks is John Turner for his assistance in deciphering the history of Terence's *Sine Cerere et Baccho friget Venus.*

Cover illustration: "Stilleben" by Abraham Mignon in the Wallraf-Richartz-Museum, Köln. Photograph source courtesy of the Rheinisches Bildarchiv, Köln.

Richard Armour's "Pickles" and "Radishes" reprinted by permission of Branden Publishing Company.

Bethami Auerbach's "The Search for the Perfect Rye Bread" from Stacy Tuthill's anthology *Rye Bread: Women Poets Rising* (College Park, Mass.: SCOP Publications). Reprinted by permission of the publisher.

Peter Beilenson's and Harry Behn's translations of "How cool the green hay" by Boncho, "If things were better" by Issa, "Oh how I enjoy" by Shiki, and "Unmoved, the melons" by Sodo from *Haiku Harvest* (Mount Vernon, N.Y.: The Peter Pauper Press). Reprinted by permission of the publisher.

Max Beerbohm's "A Luncheon" reprinted by permission of the poet's estate.

Roy Blount Jr.'s "Song Against Broccoli," "Song to Bacon," and "Song to Barbecue Sauce" from his book *One Fell Soup: Or I'm Just a Bug on the Windshield of Life.* Copyright © 1975, 1976 by Roy Blount Jr. Reprinted by permission of Little, Brown and Company.

James Broughton's "Fruits of Experience" from his book *A Long Undressing,* published by The Jargon Society. Copyright © 1971 by James Broughton. His poem "Food Food Food" has not been published previously. Both poems appear here by the kind permission of the poet.

Helen Chasin's "The Word *Plum*" from her book *Coming Close and Other Poems.* Copyright © 1968 by Yale University. Reprinted by permission of Yale University Press.

Derek Coltman's translations of "Boudin Blanc" and "The Cantaloupe" by anonymous authors and "The Peach" by Victor Hugo from Robert Courtine's *The Hundred Glories of French Cooking,* translated by Derek Coltman. Translation copyright © 1973 by Farrar, Straus & Giroux, Inc. Reprinted by permission of Farrar, Straus & Giroux, Inc.

Noel Coward's "Any Part of Piggy," copyright © by The Estate of Noel Coward, reprinted by permission of Michael Imison Playwrights Ltd., 28 Almeida Street, London N1 1TD.

Emily Dickinson's "The Mushrooms ..." from *The Poems of Emily Dickinson,* edited by Thomas H. Johnson (Cambridge, Mass.: The Belknap Press of Harvard University Press). Copyright © 1951, 1955, 1979, 1983 by the President and Fellows of Harvard College. Reprinted by permission of the publishers and Trustees of Amherst College.

Kate Flores's translation of "Pomegranates" by Paul Valéry reprinted by permission of the Angel Flores Estate.

Edgar A. Guest's "Lemon Pie" from his book *Collected Verse of Edgar A. Guest.* Copyright © 1934 by Edgar A. Guest. Reprinted by the permission of Contemporary Books, Chicago.

John Haines's "The Cauliflower" from *The Stone Harp.* Copyright © 1971 by John Haines. Published by Wesleyan University Press. Reprinted by permission of the University Press of New England.

Acknowledgments

Seamus Heaney's "Oysters" from his book *Selected Poems 1966-1987*. Copyright © 1990 by Seamus Heaney. Reprinted by permission of Farrar, Straus & Giroux, Inc.

Peter Jay's translation of "Touch, cup" by Leontios from *The Greek Anthology*, edited by Peter Jay (London: Allen Lane, 1973). Copyright © 1973 by Peter Jay. Reprinted by permission of Penguin Books Ltd.

Erica Jong's "(Artichoke, After Neruda)" and "For the taste of the fruit" from her book *Fruits & Vegetables*. Copyright © 1971 by Erica Mann Jong. Published by Holt, Rinehart & Winston. Reprinted by permission of the poet.

Denise Levertov "O Taste and See" from her book *O Taste and See*. Copyright © 1964 by Denise Levertov. Reprinted by permission of New Directions Publishing Corporation.

C. F. MacIntyre's translation of "Le Marchand d'Ail et d'Oignons" by Stéphane Mallarmé from *Stéphane Mallarmé: Selected Poems,* bilingual edition, translated and edited by C. F. MacIntyre. Reprinted by permission of the Regents of the University of California and the University of California Press.

Gerard Previn Meyer's translation of "At the Green Cabaret 5 P.M." by Arthur Rimbaud. Reprinted by permission of The Stone House Press.

Spike Milligan's "A Thousand Hairy Savages" from his book *Silly Verse for Kids*. Reprinted by permission of Penguin Books Ltd.

Edwin Morgan's translations of the three poems, entitled here as "Three Offerings," by Phillippos of Thessalonika from *The Greek Anthology*, edited by Peter Jay (London: Allen Lane, 1973). Reprinted by permission of the poet.

Paul Muldoon's "Sushi" from his book *Meeting the British*. Reprinted by permission of Wake Forest University Press.

Ogden Nash's "Celery,"* "The Eel,"† and "The Smelt"* from his book *Verses from 1929 On*. Copyright © 1941, 1942 by Ogden Nash. * First appeared in *The Saturday Evening Post*.† First appeared in *The New Yorker*. Reprinted by permission of Little, Brown and Company.

Howard Nemerov's "Manners" from his book *Sentences*. Copyright © 1980 by Howard Nemerov. Published by the University of Chicago Press. Reprinted by the permission of the poet's estate.

May Sarton's "The Fig" from her book *A Grain of Mustard Seed*. Copyright © 1971 by May Sarton. Reprinted by permission of W. W. Norton & Company.

Philip Silver's translation of Jorge Carrera Andrade's "Walnut" is from Philip Silver's *Ortega as Phenomenologist*. Copyright © 1978 by Columbia University Press, New York. Reprinted by permission of the publisher.

Stuart Terry's "Meat & Fish" has not been published previously. The poem appears here courtesy of the poet.

William Carlos Williams's "This Is Just to Say" from *William Carlos Williams: Collected Poems 1909-1939, Vol. II*. Copyright © 1938 by New Directions Publishing Corporation. Reprinted by permission of New Directions Publishing Corporation.

Adrian Wright's translation of "Every year men harvest grapes" by Macedonius from *The Greek Anthology*, edited by Peter Jay (London: Allen Lane, 1973). Reprinted by permission of the poet.

Robert Yagley's "The Tomato" has not been published previously.

Table of Contents

Table of Contents

Table of Contents

Table of Contents

Table of Contents

Table of Contents

Introduction

ince Eve partook of that fated apple, the foods that nourish mankind have always required some act of human effort. In cultivating the orchard or farm, the necessary practice, skill, and labor further the components that good soil and good climate produce. Bread, as organic as it may be, still requires deft hands and sharp eyes to combine its elements and tend the oven. From the labor of the harvest to the fruit of spiritual teachings, food as both a communal rite and a personal preference embodies more than simple necessity.

If art is, as the poet Robert Duncan comments, "an act of consciousness," the culinary art then is the embodiment of seeing food as something more than a means of survival. Even in the simplest meal, there may be fruit favored by a particular region, vegetables unique to spring or fall, or a special combination of ingredients with deep cultural or family associations. The culinary arts' relation to the poetic process may seem a minor one, but—as the poets in this volume testify—it is a fruitful relationship of long standing.

The poems gathered for this book are from sources as diverse as Peter Jay's *Greek Anthology*, a collection of *Elizabethan Verse*, and Stacy Tuthill's *Rye Bread: Women Poets Rising*, a contemporary volume of women's poetry. Placed beside one another, they blend the many regional and historical approaches to the cultivation of food. It is the purpose of *Poems from the Table* to enhance this mixture of writing and cooking, of the recipe and the poem, and of the meal and the act of reading. William Blake's adage "The Authors are in Eternity" is as welcome here as is Brillat-Savarin's philosophic note "the pleasures of the table are of all times and all ages, of every country and of every day."

As with shelter and clothing, the distribution and consumption of food forms an integral aspect of both individual lives and the body politic. Food's ability to be combined into countless meals for numerous purposes reflects the multitude of lifestyles it serves as well as the elastic nature of the human imagination, as the infinite number of recipes, cookbooks, and restaurants demonstrates. Food has been politicized by grass-roots organizations for protesting New Hampshire's Seabrook Nuclear Plant ("Acres of Clams" is an anthem for the Clamshell Alliance) and utilized for displaying one's wealth through banquets and feasts. Without the gluttony of Belshezzar's feast or the destitution of famine, *Poems from the Table* sets out to cover seven aspects of our relationship with food, fluctuating between such contrasting themes as the mundane and mythological, the self and other, and the subtle and spicy.

Together the seven parts of this book form a loosely structured narrative. It begins with THE HARVEST, whose perennial abundance gives birth to the symbol of THE CORNUCOPIA. The story then moves IN THE KITCHEN, where the take of the harvest has its organic shapes and inherent flavors enhanced, inspiring the child's imagination with MASH-POTATO CASTLES and gravy-filled moats and loosening up the tongue, feelings, and mind amid TABLE TALK. The narrative then culminates with the amorous effects of the meal in BACCHUS, CERES PLEASETH VENUS and on the divine nature of our food in SACRED FRUIT.

Within each section the themes are then embellished by the poet's fascination with the essence of food. Such poems as the "Harvest-Home Song," "Harvest Song," and "Harvest Home!" elicit cheers, applause, and song for the vitality of the worker during the harvest, while "The Solitary Reaper" and "After Apple-Picking" are songs for the dreams, memories, or ballads the harvesters recall amidst the mundane details of their work. "The Pat of Butter," "Fish Feast," and "Harvest Hymn" are songs on the various yields of the harvest, its abundance of tastes, sizes, colors, and qualities. The inventions of the blade and reaper that moved civilization from its earlier agricultural roots appear with "The Steam Threshing Machine" by Charles Tennyson, who recognizes this machine as an omnious sign of change.

From John Haines's "The Cauliflower" to Sodo's "Unmoved, the melons," THE CORNUCOPIA contains poems that illustrate the fruits of the earth simply as portraits. Though presented here as nature has given them to us, the life of vegetation at times has some very real human characteristics. The potato in the eyes of Thomas Moore is a never-say-die rebel; the peach to Victor Hugo, the touch of a woman; and to John Haines, the cauliflower is a

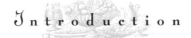

spirited, open-minded individual. Each unique to itself, these unchanging portraits here are meant to form only part of a larger picture of what this volume illustrates the cornucopia to be.

Many of the poets gathered IN THE KITCHEN write of a valid yet obscure subject matter for poetry—the recipe. We can ask, "Is this poetry?" but then what is poetry but what the Greek root of *poietria* means—"to create, to make"—the creating of phrases, thoughts, feelings, and characters that reveals the heart and soul of the matter. Here, the desire for mountain heights and treetops is found in the simpler delights of Irish stew and *boudin blanc*. The similarities between a poem and a recipe (both are read as a series of short lines from top to bottom and both utilize a combination of things in the hope of creating an impression that lasts) add some justification to the efforts of these culinary poets.

The poems of MASH-POTATO CASTLES are monuments to the child's playful energy. Like sand castles or paper hats, they have no further purpose than their own momentary amusement. Whimsical, capricious, humorous—it is no wonder many of these poems were written anonymously—they are poems created to forget about one's cares, worries, debts, and most important, one's boredom.

Whether it be dinner or lunch, the poems of TABLE TALK focus on the occasions and conversations of those taking part in a meal. Like the watering hole on a desert plain, the need for food brings together diverse company. Poems such as James Smith's "Table Talk" or Max Beerbohm's "Luncheon" see certain pairings of company best left at separate tables. Keats's "Lines on the Mermaid Tavern" extols the tavern where poets contemporary with Shakespeare and Marlowe joined together for meals and spirited talk. On the following two pages, like opening a door, we hear the Elizabethan voices of Ben Jonson and John Lyly celebrating the joy of their victuals and drink.

The other poems of TABLE TALK express their thoughts on the topic of the meal itself. It was Brillat-Savarin who said, "You are what you eat," but as William King's "What We Eat" shows, what you eat can change who you are as well. In Seamus Heaney's "Oysters," the poet feels guilty for enjoying his oysters, this "glut of privilege," but when he realizes that it might quicken him "all into verb, pure verb," this association between eating and being hastens his appetite.

The title BACCHUS, CERES PLEASETH VENUS is a loose adaptation of the Latin quote *Sine Cerere et Baccho friget Venus.* A more literal translation of this quote would be "Without Ceres and Bacchus, Venus is chilled." Though this title first appeared in Terence's play *The Eunuch*, written in 161 B.C., the poems of BACCHUS, CERES PLEASETH VENUS recall a trinity as old as the earliest civilization. For even during Terence's time, his audience would have recognized the relationship between food, drink, and love as an ancient one.

If the poems of the previous section remind us of the relationship between food and the body, the poems of SACRED FRUIT describe the correspondence between the fruits of the earth and the blossoming of the soul. The leaves, flowers, and fruit that return to the trees seem even more sublime with each passing winter. Thus, the flowering spring that once produced romance now signals the well-being of the spirit. Here the image is of the reaper as Old Father Time sitting near a sundial beside the ruins of a cloister or abbey. The seeds planted in youth have hopefully borne fruit in the actions of our adult lives, now harvested as memories. Though his robe is worn and his arms thin, the wisdom of Old Father Time is golden.

With the meals and songs of Thanksgiving at year's end coupled with Father Time as the reaper, *Poems from the Table*, circular like the seasons, ends where it began—with allusions to THE HARVEST. So those readers who return to the first poems of this book and start this narrative again will find themselves in rhythm with the harvester, poet, cook, child, dandy, lover, and philosopher all conversing at one table. Or memorizing these poems, the reader may repeat them again while preparing a meal, passing an orchard, or speaking intimately to another. For like a spring wind or a scent of fresh apple pie, the verses herein bring to mind such pleasant omens.

—*Robert Yagley*
1995

The Harvest

O TASTE AND SEE

The world is
not with us enough.
O taste and see

the subway Bible poster said,
meaning **The Lord,** meaning
if anything all that lives
to the imagination's tongue,

grief, mercy, language,
tangerine, weather, to
breathe them, bite,
savor, chew, swallow, transform

into our flesh our
deaths, crossing the street, plum, quince,
living in the orchard and being

hungry, and plucking
the fruit.

Denise Levertov

From TO AUTUMN

S eason of mists and mellow fruitfulness,
    Close bosom-friend of the maturing sun;
Conspiring with him how to load and bless
    With fruit the vines that round the thatch-eaves run;
To bend with apples the moss'd cottage-trees,
    And fill all fruit with ripeness to the core;
        To swell the gourd, and plump the hazel shells
    With a sweet kernel; to set budding more,
And still more, later flowers for the bees,
Until they think warm days will never cease,
        For Summer has o'er-brimm'd their clammy cells.

Who hath not seen thee oft amid thy store?
    Sometimes whoever seeks abroad may find
Thee sitting careless on a granary floor,
    Thy hair soft-lifted by the winnowing wind;
Or on a half-reap'd furrow sound asleep,
    Drows'd with the fume of poppies, while thy hook
        Spares the next swath and all its twined flowers:
And sometimes like a gleaner thou dost keep
    Steady thy laden head across a brook;
    Or by a cider-press, with patient look,
        Thou watchest the last oozings, hours by hours.

John Keats

The Harvest

HARVEST-HOME SONG

The frost will bite us soon;
    His tooth is on the leaves:
Beneath the golden moon
    We bear the golden sheaves:
We care not for the winter's spite,
We keep our Harvest-home to-night.
        Hurrah for the English yeoman!
        Fill full, fill the cup!
        Hurrah! he yields to no man!
        Drink deep; drink it up!

The pleasure of a king
    Is tasteless to the mirth
Of peasants when they bring
    The harvest of the earth.
With pipe and tabor hither roam
All ye who love our Harvest-home.

The thresher with his flail,
    The shepherd with his crook,
The milkmaid with her pail,
    The reaper with his hook—
To-night the dullest blooded clods
Are kings and queens, are demigods.
        Hurrah for the English yeoman!
        Fill full; fill the cup!
        Hurrah! he yields to no man!
        Drink deep; drink it up!

John Davidson

Poems from the Table

From HARVEST SONG

I love, I love to see
   Bright steel gleam through the land;
'Tis a goodly sight, but it must be
   In the reaper's tawny hand.

I love to see the field
   That is moist with purple stain;
But not where bullet, sword, and shield
   Lie strewn with the gory slain.

No, no; 'tis where the sun
   Shoots down his cloudless beams,
Till rich and bursting juice-drops run
   On the vineyard earth in streams.

My glowing heart beats high
   At the sight of shining gold;
But it is not that which the miser's eye
   Delighteth to behold.

A brighter wealth by far,
   Than the deep mine's yellow vein,
Is seen around in the fair hills crowned
   With sheaves of burnished grain.

The Harvest

The feast that Nature gives
　　Is not for one alone;
'Tis shared by the meanest slave that lives
　　And the tenant of a throne.

Then glory to the steel
　　That shines in the reaper's hand.
And thanks to Him who has blest the seed,
　　And crowned the harvest land.

　　　　　Eliza Cook

THE STEAM THRESHING MACHINE

Did any seer of ancient time forbode
This mighty engine, which we daily see
Accepting our full harvests, like a god,
With clouds about his shoulders,—it might be
Some poet-husbandman, some lord of verse,
Old Hesiod, or the wizard Mantuan
Who catalogued in rich hexameters
The Rake, the Roller, and the mystic Van:
Or else some priest of Ceres, it might seem,
Who witnessed, as he trod the silent fane,
The notes and auguries of coming change,
Of other ministrants in shrine and grange,
The sweating statue,—and her sacred wain
Low-booming with the prophecy of steam!

　　　　　Charles Tennyson

THE SOLITARY REAPER

*B*ehold her, single in the field,
Yon solitary Highland Lass!
Reaping and singing by herself;
Stop here, or gently pass!
Alone she cuts and binds the grain,
And sings a melancholy strain;
O listen! for the Vale profound
Is overflowing with the sound.

No Nightingale did ever chaunt
More welcome notes to weary bands
Of travelers in some shady haunt,
Among Arabian sands:
A voice so thrilling ne'er was heard
In spring-time from the Cuckoo-bird,
Breaking the silence of the seas
Among the farthest Hebrides.

Will no one tell me what she sings?—
Perhaps the plaintive numbers flow
For old, unhappy, far-off things,
And battles long ago:
Or is it some more humble lay,
Familiar matter of today?
Some natural sorrow, loss, or pain,
That has been, and may be again?

What'er the theme, the Maiden sang
As if her song could have no ending;
I saw her singing at her work,

The Harvest

And o'er the sickle bending:—
I listened, motionless and still;
And, as I mounted up the hill,
The music in my heart I bore,
Long after it was heard no more.

William Wordsworth

UNDER THE HARVEST MOON

Under the harvest moon,
When the soft silver
Drips shimmering
Over the garden nights,
Death, the gray mocker,
Comes and whispers to you
As a beautiful friend
Who remembers.

Under the summer roses
When the flagrant crimson
Lurks in the dusk
Of the wild red leaves,
Love, with little hands,
Comes and touches you
With a thousand memories,
And asks you
Beautiful, unanswerable questions.

Carl Sandburg

AFTER APPLE-PICKING

My long two-pointed ladder's sticking through a tree
Toward heaven still,
And there's a barrel that I didn't fill
Beside it, and there may be two or three
Apples I didn't pick upon some bough.
But I am done with apple-picking now.
Essence of winter sleep is on the night,
The scent of apples: I am drowsing off.
I cannot rub the strangeness from my sight
I got from looking through a pane of glass
I skimmed this morning from the drinking trough
And held against the world of hoary grass.
It melted, and I let it fall and break.
But I was well
Upon my way to sleep before it fell,
And I could tell
What form my dreaming was about to take.
Magnified apples appear and disappear,
Stem end and blossom end,
And every fleck of russet showing clear.
My instep arch not only keeps the ache,
It keeps the pressure of a ladder-round.
I feel the ladder sway as the boughs bend.
And I keep hearing from the cellar bin
The rumbling sound
Of load on load of apples coming in.
For I have had too much
Of apple-picking: I am overtired
Of the great harvest I myself desired.
There were ten thousand thousand fruit to touch,

Cherish in hand, lift down, and not let fall.
For all
That struck the earth,
No matter if not bruised or spiked with stubble,
Went surely to the cider-apple heap
As of no worth.
One can see what will trouble
This sleep of mine, whatever sleep it is.
Were he not gone,
The woodchuck could say whether it's like his
Long sleep, as I describe its coming on,
Or just some human sleep.

Robert Frost

How cool the green hay
    Smells, carried in
    Through the farm gate
At sunshine!

Boncho
Translated from the Japanese by
Peter Beilenson and Harry Behn

THE LAPFUL OF NUTS

Whene'er I see soft hazel eyes
    And nut-brown curls,
I think of those bright days I spent
    Among the Limerick girls;
When up through Cratla woods I went,
    Nutting with thee;
And we pluck'd the glossy clustering fruit
    From a many bending tree.

Beneath the hazel boughs we sat,
    Thou, love, and I,
And the gather'd nuts lay in thy lap,
    Beneath thy downcast eye:
But little we thought of the store we'd won,
    I, love, or thou;
For our hearts were full, and we dare not own
    The love that's spoken now.

Oh, there's wars for willing hearts in Spain,
    And high Germaine!
And I'll come back, ere long, again,
    With knightly fame and fee:
And I'll come back, if I ever come back,
    Faithful to thee,
That sat with thy white lap full of nuts
    Beneath the hazel tree.

Samuel Ferguson

THE PAT OF BUTTER

Once, at the Agricultural Show,
We tasted–all so yellow—
Those butter-pats, cool and mellow!
Each taste I still remember, though
It was so long ago.

This spoke of the grass of Netherhay,
And this of Kingcomb Hill,
And this of Coker Rill:
Which was the prime I could not say
Of all those tried that day,

Till she, the fair and wicked-eyed,
Held out a pat to me:
Then felt I all Yeo-Lea
Was by her sample sheer outvied;
And, "This is the best," I cried.

Thomas Hardy

HERRINGS FINE!

Out of the heaving dusk, toward the pier,
With sun in heart, and sunrise on each keel,
The herring boats flock home for morning meal;
Above the rosy rooftrees, as they near,
The blue smoke curls. They close their wings and steer
With labouring oar; they catch the loud appeal
Of loungers, asking of their woe or weal,
The children's laughter, and the fishwives' cheer.
Scaled o'er with silver, see, the skipper stands,
While the loud bell proclaims the sample fair;
Moveless of lip, he hears his net's supply
Measured against a nation's whole demands;
And soon the town takes up the joyous cry,
And "Herrings fine!" is ringing thro' the air.

Hardwick Drummond Rawnsley

FISH FEAST

All day we sat, until the sun went down—
'Twas summer, and the Dog-star scorch'd the Town—
At fam'd Blackwall, O Thames! upon thy shore,
Where Lovegrove's tables groan beneath their store,
We feasted full, on every famous dish,
Dress'd many ways, of sea and river fish—
Perch, mullet, eels, and salmon, all were there,
And whitebait, daintiest of our fishy fare—
Then meat of various kinds, and venison last,
Quails, fruits and ices, crown'd the rich repast.
Thy fields, Champagne, supplied us with our wine,
Madeira's island, and the rocks of Rhine.
The sun was set, and twilight veil'd the land:
Then all stood up—all who had strength to stand—
And pouring down, of Maraschino, fit
Libations to the gods of wine and wit,
In steam-wing'd chariots and on iron roads
Sought the great City, and our own abodes.

Thomas Love Peacock

ACRES OF CLAMS

I've traveled all over this country,
Prospecting and digging for gold.
I've tunneled, hydraulicked and cradled,
And, I have been frequently sold.

First Chorus:
And I have been frequently sold, *(repeat)*
I've tunneled, hydraulicked and cradled,
And, I have been frequently sold.

For one who gets riches by mining
Perceiving that hundreds grow poor,
I made up my mind to try farming,
The only pursuit that is sure.

Second Chorus:
The only pursuit that is sure, *(repeat)*
I made up mind to try farming
The only pursuit that is sure.

So, rolling my grub in my blanket,
I left all my tools on the ground,
And started one morning to shank it
For a country they call Puget Sound.

Third Chorus:
For a country they call Puget Sound, *(repeat)*
And started one morning to shank it
For a country they call Puget Sound.

The Harvest

No longer the slave of ambition,
I laugh at the world and its shams,
And I think of my happy condition
Surrounded by acres of clams.

Fourth Chorus:
Surrounded by acres of clams, *(repeat)*
And think of my happy condition
Surrounded by acres of clams.

Anonymous

HARVEST HOME!

The last golden sheaf is borne off from the meadow,
  The reaper is gone for his labour is done;
The harvest that grew where no cloud threw its shadow
  Was gathered to-day in the smiles of the sun.
        See! see! the tankard's foam!
        Hark! hark! 'tis harvest home!

Youth trips to the sound of the pipe and the tabor,
  While innocent childhood looks on with his laugh,
And happy old age tells some listening neighbour
  Of festivals past, as he leans on his staff.
        See! see! the tankard's foam!
        Hark! hark! 'tis harvest home!

Nathaniel Thomas Haynes Bayly

From HARVEST HYMN

Whoever fails, Thou dost not fail;
    Whoever sleeps, Thou dost not sleep;
With fattening shower, and fostering gale,
    Thy mercy brings the time to reap;
Man marks each season and its sign,
    And sows the seed and plants the tree,
But form, growth, fulness, all are Thine,—
    Lord of the harvest, praise to Thee!

O God! it is a pleasant thing
    To see the precious grain expand,
And the broad hands of Plenty fling
    Her golden largess o'er the land;
To see the fruitage swell and glow,
    And bow with wealth the parent tree;
To see the purple vintage flow—
    Lord of abundance, praise to Thee!

Praise for the glorious harvest days,
    And all the blessings that we share;
For the unbounded sunlight praise
    And for the free and vital air;
Praise for the faith that looks above;
    The hope of immortality;
For life, health, virtue, truth and love,
    Maker and Giver, praise to Thee!

John Critchley Prince

The Cornucopia

THE CAULIFLOWER

I wanted to be a cauliflower,
all brain and ears,
thinking on the origin of gardens
and the divinity of him
who carefully binds my leaves.

With my blind roots touched
by the songs of the worms,
and my rough throat throbbing
with strange, vegetable sounds,
perhaps I'd feel the parting stroke
of a butterfly's wing . . .

Not like my cousins, the cabbages,
whose heads, tightly folded,
see and hear nothing of this world,
dreaming only on the yellow
and green magnificence
that is hardening within them.

John Haines

Poems from the Table

POMEGRANATES

Les Grenades

Hard pomegranates sundered
By excess of your seeds,
You make me think of mighty brows
Aburst with their discoveries!

If the suns you underwent,
O pomegranates severed,
Wrought your essence with the pride
To rend your ruby segments,

And if the dry gold of your shell
At instance of a power
Cracks in crimson gems of juice,

This luminous eruption
Sets a soul to dream upon
Its secret architecture.

Paul Valéry
Translated from the French by Kate Flores

"THE MUSHROOMS . . ."

The Mushrooms is the Elf of Plants—
At Evening, it is not—
At Morning, in a Truffled Hut
It stop upon a Spot

As if it tarried always
And yet its whole Career
Is shorter than a Snake's Delay
And fleeter than a Tare[1]—

'Tis Vegetation's Juggler—
The Germ of Alibi—
Doth like a Bubble antedate
And like a Bubble, hie—

I feel as if the Grass was pleased
To have it intermit—
This surreptitious scion
Of Summer's circumspect.

Had Nature any supple Face
Or could she one contemn—
Had Nature an Apostate—
That Mushroom—it is Him!

Emily Dickinson

1. A weed, member of the vetch family

THE HONEYCOMB

If thou hast found an honeycomb,
Eat thou not all, but taste on some;
For if thou eat'st it to excess,
That sweetness turns to loathsomeness.
Taste it to temper; then 'twill be
Marrow and manna unto thee.

Robert Herrick

THE CANTALOUPE

Though on the tongue its melting yields
A taste with heavenly sweetness graced,
It sometimes of the pumpkin feels—
It has that faded tint and taste.

Anonymous
Translated from the French by Derek Coltman

WALNUT

Walnut: compressed wisdom,
Tiny vegetable turtle,
Brain of an elf
Paralyzed for eternity.

Jorge Carrera Andrade
Translated from the Spanish by Philip Silver

The Cornucopia

From BLUEBERRIES

You ought to have seen what I saw on my way
To the village, through Patterson's pasture to-day:
Blueberries as big as the end of your thumb,
Real sky-blue, and heavy, and ready to drum
In the cavernous pail of the first one to come!
And all ripe together, not some of them green
And some of them ripe! You ought to have seen!'

'I don't know what part of the pasture you mean.'

'You know where they cut off the woods—let me see—
It was two years ago—or no!—can it be
No longer than that?—and the following fall
The fire ran and burned it all up but the wall.'

'Why, there hasn't been time for the bushes to grow.
That's always the way with the blueberries, though:
There may not have been the ghost of a sign
Of them anywhere under the shade of the pine,
But get the pine out of the way, you may burn
The pasture all over until not a fern
Or grass-blade is left, not to mention a stick,
And presto, they're up all around you as thick
And hard to explain as a conjuror's trick.'

'It must be on charcoal they fatten their fruit.
I taste in them sometimes the flavour of soot.
And after all really they're ebony skinned:

The blue's but a mist from the breath of the wind,
A tarnish that goes at a touch of the hand,
And less than the tan with which pickers are tanned.'

Robert Frost

THE FIG

Under the green leaf hangs a little pouch
Shaped like a gourd, purple and leathery.
It fits the palm, it magnetizes touch.
What flesh designed as fruit can this fruit be?

The plump skin gives a little at the seam.
Now bite it deep for better or for worse!
Oh multitude of stars, pale green and crimson—
And you have dared to eat a universe!

May Sarton

ASPARAGUS

Ripe 'sparagrass,
Fit for lad or lass,
To make their water pass:
Oh, 'tis pretty picking
With a tender chicken!

Jonathan Swift

OYSTERS

Charming oysters I cry:
My masters, come buy.
So plump and so fresh,
So sweet is their flesh,
No Colchester oyster
Is sweeter and moister:
Your stomach they settle,
And rouse up your mettle;
They'll make you a dad
Of a lass or a lad;
And madam your wife
They'll please to the life;
Be she barren, be she old,
Be she slut, or be she scold,
Eat my oysters, and lie near her,
She'll be fruitful, never fear her.

Jonathan Swift

Poems from the Table

THE PEACH

This fruit seduces all men's eyes
And all their senses gratifies;
Its velvet cool our touch can teach
How roses may be blent with lilies;
This golden form could well be Phyllis . . .
Were it not a tender peach.

> Victor Hugo
> *Translated from the French by Derek Coltman*

THE POTATO

I'm a careless potato, and care not a pin
    How into existence I came;
If they planted me drill-wise, or dibbled me in,
    To me 't is exactly the same.
The bean and the pea may more loftily tower,
    But I care not a button for them;
Defiance I nod with my beautiful flower
    When the earth is hoed up to my stem.

> Thomas Moore

THE TOMATO

We do not recognize
fully, a tomato,
when it is green.

It is something else.
We call it—
unready, not yet . . .

The earth, we admit,
has not fully found its way.

The fruitless color of its
stems, leaves, and buds,
still runs in its gift.

Youth's exuberance
overflowing, maybe, but it is
not yet, we say,

a tomato.

Robert Yagley

THE SMELT

Oh, why does man pursue the smelt?
It has no valuable pelt,
It boasts of no escutcheon royal,
It yields no ivory or oil,
Its life is dull, its death is tame.
A fish as humble as its name
Yet—take this salmon somewhere else.
And bring me half a dozen smelts.

Ogden Nash

THE HERB

Herb Duty in life's common ground hath root;
Joy its sweet flow'r, Content its wholesome fruit.

William Allingham

Unmoved, the melons
        Don't seem to recall
        One drop
Of last night's downpour

Sodo
*Translated from the Japanese by Peter Beilenson
and Harry Behn*

In the Kitchen

IRISH STEW

Irish stew, Irish stew!
    Whatever else my dinner be,
Once again, once again,
    I'd have a dish of thee.
Mutton chops, and onion slice,
    Let the water cover,
With potatoes, fresh and nice;
    Boil, but not quite over,
        Irish stew, Irish stew!
Ne'er from thee, my taste will stray.
        I could eat
        Such a treat
Nearly every day.
        La, la, la, la!

From Punch

OATMEAL PUDDING

Of oats decorticated take two pound,
And of new milk enough the same to drown;
Of raisins of the sun, ston'd, ounces eight;
Of currants, cleanly pick'd, an equal weight;
Of suet, finely slic'd, an ounce at least;
And six eggs newly taken from the nest:
Season this mixture well with salt and spice;
'Twill make a pudding far exceeding rice;
And you may safely feed on it like farmers,
For the receipt is learned Dr. Harmer's.

William King

GOURDS

First cut the gourds in slices, and then run
Threads through their breadth, and dry them in the air;
Then smoke them hanging them above the fire;
So that the slaves may in the winter season
Take a large dish and fill it with the slices,
And feast on them on holidays: meanwhile
Let the cook add all sorts of vegetables,
And throw them seed and all into the dish;
Let them take strings of gherkins fairly wash'd,
And mushrooms, and all sorts of herbs in bunches,
And curly cabbages, and add them too.

Nicander
Translated from the Greek by Charles Duke Yonge

In the Kitchen

From THE BALLAD OF BOUILLABAISSE

A street there is in Paris famous,
  For which no rhyme our language yields,
Rue Neuve des petits Champs its name is—
  The New Street of the Little Fields;
And there's an inn, not rich and splendid,
  But still in comfortable case—
The which in youth I oft attended,
  To eat a bowl of Bouillabaisse.

This Bouillabaisse a noble dish is—
  A sort of soup, or broth, or brew,
Or hotchpotch of all sorts of fishes,
  That Greenwich never could outdo;
Green herbs, red peppers, mussels, saffern,
  Soles, onions, garlic, roach, and dace;
All these you eat at Terré's tavern,
  In that one dish of Bouillabaisse.

❪ ❪ ❪

I drink it as the Fates ordain it.
  Come, fill it, and have done with rhymes;
Fill up the lonely glass, and drain it
  In memory of dear old times.
Welcome the wine, whate'er the seal is;
  And sit you down and say your grace
With thankful heart, whate'er the meal is.
  —Here comes the smoking Bouillabaisse!

William Makepeace Thackeray

From THE SEARCH FOR THE PERFECT RYE BREAD

The perfect rye bread
has not been found
but every near-miss
every changeling
emerging from my oven
is savored;
nothing I make
with my own hands
can be all bad.

It's a long time to be housebound
    researching
    organizing
    measuring
    mixing
    kneading
    rising
    baking
    cooling
    tasting
4 hours at least
sometimes 6
But these are hours

when something is going on in my life,
hours when I might be home
staring at my hands
in terror that nothing is going on in my life.

In the Kitchen

These are hours of ferment
when, after washing my spoon,
I might grab my pen;
hours of waiting
for a sign
that I can make something
out of nothing.

Bethami Auerbach

THIS IS JUST TO SAY

I have eaten
the plums
that were in
the icebox

and which
you were probably
saving
for breakfast

Forgive me
they were delicious
so sweet
and so cold

William Carlos Williams

Poems from the Table

ON COOKBOOKS

*T*is a sage Question, if the Art of Cooks
Is lodg'd by Nature, or attain'd by Books:
That Man will never frame a noble Treat
Whose whole Dependance lies on some Receipt.
Then by pure Nature ev'ry thing is spoil'd,
She knows no more than stew'd, bak'd, roast and boil'd.
When Art and Nature join th' Effect will be
Some nice Ragout, or charming Fricassee.

William King

"AMELIA MIXED THE MUSTARD"

A melia mixed the mustard,
    She mixed it good and thick;
She put it in the custard
    And made her Mother sick,
And showing satisfaction
    By many a loud huzza
'Observe' said she 'the action
    Of mustard on Mamma.'

A. E. Housman

From CYRANO DE BERGERAC

"How to make tartelettes amandines"

Beat some eggs until
there's froth and foam;
then into this mix, blend
a tangy citron juice
and the finest almond
milk you can use.

Now, line your pans and place
some light pastry dough,
with just a hint
of brandied apricot
about the rim.

Then drop by drop,
slowly pour your foam
until you fill them,
then in the oven bake 'em,
'til a golden brown—
Now sit down—
it's a merry sight to see—
Your *tartelettes amandines!*

Edmond Rostand
Translated from the French by Bob Thorne

From BOILED CHICKEN

Lesbia, take some cold water,
    And having on the fire placed it,
And some butter, and be bold—
    When 'tis hot enough—taste it.
Oh! the Chicken meant for me
    Boil before the fire grows dimmer;
Twenty minutes let it be
    In the saucepan left to simmer.
            Oh, my tender Chicken dear!
My boil'd, delicious, tender Chicken.
            Rub the breast
            (To give a zest)
With lemon-juice, my tender Chicken.

Lesbia hath with sauce combined
    Broccoli white, without a tarnish;
'Tis hard to tell if 'tis design'd
    For vegetable or for garnish.
Pillow'd on a butter'd dish,
    My Chicken temptingly reposes,
    Making gourmands for it wish,
    Should the savor reach their noses.
            Oh, my tender pullet dear!
My boiled—not roasted—tender Chicken!
            Day or night,
            Thy meal is light.
For supper, e'en, my tender Chicken.

From Punch

In the Kitchen

SONG TO BACON

Consumer groups have gone and taken
Some of the savor out of bacon.
Protein-per-penny in bacon, they say,
Equals needles-per-square-inch of hay.
Well, I know, after cooking all
That's left to eat is mighty small
    (You also get a lot of lossage
      In life, romance, and country sausage),
And I will vote for making it cheaper,
Wider, longer, leaner, deeper,
But let's not throw the baby, please,
Out with the (visual rhyme here) grease.
There's nothing crumbles like bacon still,
And I don't think there ever will
Be anything, whate'er you use
For meat, that chews like bacon chews.
And also: I wish these groups would tell
Me whether they counted in the smell.
The smell of it cooking's worth $2.10 a pound.
And howbout the *sound*?

Roy Blount Jr.

BOUDIN BLANC

Chop onions fine, and on flame not high
With equal part of bacon fry.
Toss till onion is a golden color
And kitchen filled with sweet aroma.
Mix with the blood and season well
With pepper, salt, and spice as well.
A glass of brandy add, then fill
A pig's intestine, though not until
One end's been tied. When all your paste
Is safely in, and both ends laced,
Cook twenty minutes, or thereabout,
In simmering water, then hoist out.
      Now by the yule log's crackling blaze
      Inviting you to stretch and laze
      Reap the reward of all your toil
      And watch your *boudins* gently broil.

Anonymous
Translated from the French by Derek Coltman

SONG TO BARBECUE SAUCE

Hot and sweet and red and greasy,
I could eat a gallon easy:
Barbecue sauce!
Lay it on, hoss.

Nothing is dross
Under barbecue sauce.

Brush it on chicken, slosh it on pork,
Eat it with fingers, not with a fork.
I could eat barbecued turtle or squash—
I could eat tar paper cooked and awash
In barbecue sauce.

I'd eat Spanish moss
With barbecue sauce.

Hear this from Evelyn Billiken Husky,
Formerly Evelyn B. of Sandusky:
"Ever since locating down in the South,
I have had barbecue sauce on my mouth."

Nothing can gloss
Over barbecue sauce.

Roy Blount Jr.

From A BANQUET

Avoiding all such roasts as want a spit,
I bought too some fine mullet, and young thrushes,
And put them on the coals just as they were,
Adding a little brine and marjoram.
To these I added cuttle-fish and squills.
A fine dish is the squill when carefully cook'd.
But the rich cuttle-fish is eaten plain,
Though I did stuff them with a rich forced meat
Of almost every kind of herb and flower.
Then there were several dishes of boil'd meats,
And sauce-boats full of oil and vinegar.
Besides all this a conger fine and fat
I bought, and buried in a fragrant pickle;
Likewise some tench, and clinging to the rocks
Some limpets. All their heads I tore away,
And cover'd them with flour and bread crumbs over,
And then prepared them as I dress'd the squills.
There was a widow'd amia too, a noble
And dainty fish. That did I wrap in fig-leaves,
And soak'd it through with oil, and over all
With swaddling clothes of marjoram did I fold it,
And hid it like a torch beneath the ashes.
With it I took anchovies from Phalerum,
And pour'd on them one cruet full of water.
Then shredding herbs quite fine I add more oil,
More than two cotylae in quantity.
What next? That's all. This sir is what I do,
Not learning from recipes or books of cookery.

Sotades
Translated from the Greek by Charles Duke Yonge

A RECEIPT FOR STEWING VEAL

with Notes by the Author

Take a knuckle of veal;
　　You may buy it, or steal.
In a few pieces cut it:
In a stewing-pan put it.
Salt, pepper, and mace,
　　Must season this knuckle;
Then what's join'd to a place[1]
　　With other herbs muckle;
That which killed king Will;[2]
And what never stands still.[3]
Some sprigs[4] of that bed
Where children are bred,
Which much will you mend, if
Both spinnage and endive,
And lettuce, and beet,
With marygold meet.
Put no water at all;
For it maketh things small,
Which, lest it should happen,
A close cover clap on.
Put this pot of Wood's metal[5]
In a hot boiling kettle,
and there let it be
　　(Mark the doctrine I teach)

1. Vulgo, salary. 2. Supposed sorrel. 3. This is by Dr. Bentley
thought to be time, or thyme. 4. Parsley. Vide Chamberlayne.
5. Of this composition, see the works of the Copper-farthing Dean.

About—let me see—
    Thrice as long as you preach;[6]
So skimming the fat off,
Say grace with your hat off.
O, then! with what rapture
Will it fill dean and chapter!

John Gay

6. Which we suppose to be near four hours.

From THE ART OF COOKERY

We shou'd submit our Treats to Critics View,
And ev'ry prudent Cook shou'd read *Bossu.*[1]
Judgment provides the Meat in Season fit,
Which by the Genius dress'd, its Sauce is Wit.
Good Beef for Men, Pudding for Youth and Age,
Come up to the Decorum of the Stage.
The Critic strikes out all that is not just,
And 'tis ev'n so the Butler chips his Crust.
Poets and Pastry Cooks will be the same,
Since both of them their Images must frame.
Chimera's from the Poet's Fancy flow,
The Cook contrives his Shapes in real Dough.

William King

1. Most likely Jacques Bossuet (1627–1704), great French orator
and powerful critic of his era.

Mash-Potato Castles

Mash-Potato Castles

PEAS

I eat my peas with honey,
I've done it all my life,
They do taste kind of funny,
But it keeps them on the knife.

Anonymous

"IF ALL THE WORLD . . ."

If all the world were apple pie,
    And all the sea were ink,
And all the trees were bread and cheese,
    What *should* we have to drink?

Anonymous

SONG AGAINST BROCCOLI

The neighborhood stores are all out of broccoli,
Loccoli.

Roy Blount Jr.

"WHAT'S YOUR NAME?"

What's your name?
Pudden Tame.
What's your other?
Bread and Butter.
Where do you live?
In a sieve.
What's your number?
Cucumber.

Anonymous

"DO YOU CARROT ALL FOR ME?"

Do you carrot all for me?
My heart beets for you,
With your turnip nose
And your radish face.

You are a peach.
If we canteloupe
Lettuce marry;
Weed make a swell pear.

Anonymous

A VEGETATION TO BE READ
BY THE PARSNIP

Aubergine aubergine
Lettuce pray for the marrow
For no one radishes the end
We have all cucumbered our unworthy chives
With foul swedes
It ill beetroots us to publicly sprout pea
From the endive our fennels
None escapes the cabbages of thyme
Even the wisest sage comes to a spinach
Celery celery I say unto you
This is the cauliflower
When salsifiers all
Artichoke and kale.

B. C. Leale

CELERY

Celery, raw,
Develops the jaw,
But celery, stewed,
Is more quickly chewed.

Ogden Nash

THE HERRING

The Herring he loves the merry moonlight
  And the Mackerel loves the wind,
But the Oyster loves the dredging song
  For he comes of a gentler kind.

Sir Walter Scott

A FANCY

When Piecrust first began to reign,
  Cheese-parings went to war,
Red Herrings lookt both blue and wan,
  Green Leeks and Puddings jar.
Blind Hugh went out to see
  Two cripples run a race,
The Ox fought with the Humble Bee
  And claw'd him by the face.

Anonymous

ON TOMATO KETCHUP

If you do not shake the bottle,
None'll come, and then a lot'll.

Anonymous

FOOD FOOD FOOD

A Digestible Song

Munch munch munch
with jaw saliva and crunch
some edible breadable dish
for breakfast dinner or lunch.
Has anything tastier ever been chewed
than food food food?

Was there ever a juicier joy
than something meatily sweet
that's toasted or baked or stewed
to an aromatical heat
and served in the succulent shape
of food food food?

Munch munch munch
every day for dinner or lunch
some savory flavory treat
with a drink that's icy or brewed.
Is there anything anywhere better to eat
than food food food?

James Broughton

From THE JUMBLIES

They sailed to the Wester Sea, they did—
    To a land all covered with trees:
And they bought an owl, and a useful cart,
And a pound of rice, and a cranberry-tart,
    And a hive of silvery bees;
And they bought a pig, and some green jackdaws,
And a lovely monkey with lollipop paws,
And forty bottles of ring-bo-ree,
    And no end of Stilton cheese.
        Far and few, far and few,
           Are the lands where the Jumblies live:
           Their heads are green and their hands are blue;
           And they went to sea in a sieve.

Edward Lear

From THE BOOK OF NONSENSE

Many People Seem to Think
    Plaster o' Paris
    Good to Drink;
Though Goodness unto Quiet,
I Prefer Another Diet!

Gelett Burgess

Mash-Potato Castles

A THOUSAND HAIRY SAVAGES

A thousand hairy savages
Sitting down to lunch
Gobble gobble gulp gulp
Munch munch munch.

Spike Milligan

"LIFE IS BUTTER"

Life is Butter, Life is Butter;
Melancholy flower, Melancholy flower;
Life is but a Melon, Life is but a Melon;
Cauliflower, Cauliflower.

Anonymous

MEAT & FISH

I

Mommy told us the butcher had run out of liver,
restoring our *joie de viver*.

II

I finally finished last week's tuna.
Wish I'd eaten it soona.

Stuart Terry

THE PRODIGAL EGG

An egg of humble sphere
    By vain ambition stung,
Once left his mother dear
    When he was very young.

'Tis needless to dilate
    Upon a tale so sad;
The egg, I grieve to state,
    Grew very, very bad.

At last when old and blue,
    He wandered home, and then
They gently broke it to
    The loving mother hen.

She only said, in fun,
"I fear you're spoiled, my son!"

Anonymous

EAT WITH CARE

Hocus Pocus,
Fish-bones choke us.

Anonymous

Table Talk

TABLE TALK

To weave a culinary clue,
When to eschew, and what to chew,
    Where shun, and where take rations,
I sing. Attend, ye diners-out,
And, if my numbers please you, shout
    "Hear, hear!" in acclamations.

There are who treat you, once a year,
To the same stupid set; good cheer
    Such hardship cannot soften.
To listen to the self-same dunce,
At the same leaden table, once
    Per annum's once too often.

Rather than that, mix on my plate
With men I like the meat I hate—
    Colman with pig and treacle;
Luttrell with ven'son-pasty join,
Lord Normanby with orange wine,
    And rabbit-pie with Jekyll.

Add to George Lambe a sable snipe,
Conjoin with Captain Morris tripe
    By parsley-roots made denser;
Mix Macintosh with mack'rel, with
Calves-head and bacon Sidney Smith,
    And mutton-broth with Spencer.

Poems from the Table

Shun sitting next the wight whose drone
Bores, *sotto voce*, you alone
    With flat colloquial pressure;
Debarr'd from general talk, you droop
Beneath his buzz, from orient Soup
    To occidental Cheshire.

He who can only talk with one,
Should stay at home and talk with none—
    At all events, to strangers,
Like village epitaphs of yore,
He ought to cry "Long time I bore,"
    To warn them of their dangers.

Others there are who but retail
Their breakfast journal, now grown stale,
    In print ere day was dawning;
When folks like these sit next to me,
They send me dinnerless to tea;
    One cannot chew while yawning.

Seat not good talkers one next one,
As Jacquier beards the Clarendon;
    Thus shrouded you undo 'em;
Rather confront them, face to face,
Like Holles Street and Harewood Place,
    And let the town run through 'em.

Table Talk

Poets are dangerous to sit nigh;
You waft their praises to the sky,
    And when you think you're stirring
Their gratitude, they bite you—(That's
The reason I object to cats;
    They scratch amid their purring.)

For those who ask you if you "malt,"
Who "beg your pardon" for the salt,
    And ape our upper grandees,
By wondering folks can touch port wine;
That, reader, 's your affair, not mine;
    I never mess with dandies.

          🐦   🐦   🐦

Some aim to tell a thing that hit
Where last they dined; what there was wit,
    Here meets rebuffs and crosses.
Jokes are like trees; their place of birth
Best suits them; stuck in foreign earth,
    They perish in the process.

Think, reader, of the few who groan
For any ailments save their own;
    The world, from peer to peasant,
Is heedless of your cough or gout;
Then pr'ythee, when you next dine out,
    Go arm'd with something pleasant.

                    James Smith

BREAKFAST WITH
GERARD MANLEY HOPKINS[1]

Delicious heart-of-the-corn, fresh-from-the-oven
flakes are sparkled and spangled with sugar for
a can't-be-resisted flavour.
—Legend on a packet of breakfast cereal

Serious over my cereals I broke one breakfast my fast
    With something-to-read–searching retinas retained by print on a
      packet;
Sprung rhythm sprang, and I found (the mind fact-mining at last)
    An influence Father-Hopkins–fathered on the copy-writing
      racket.

Parenthesis-proud, bracket-bold, happiest with hyphens,
    The writers stagger intoxicated by terms, adjective-unsteadied—
Describing in graceless phrases fizzling like soda siphons
    All things, crisp, crunchy, malted, tangy, sugared and shredded.

Far too, yes, too early we are urged to be purged, to savour
    Salt, malt and phosphates in English twisted and torn,
As, sparkled and spangled with sugar for a can't-be-resisted flavour,
    Come from-from-the-oven flakes direct from the heart of the
      corn.

Anthony Brode

1. Hopkins (1844-1889) was a Jesuit priest and poet of dazzling verbal
gifts. He called his unusual metrical system "sprung rhythm."

A LUNCHEON

(Thomas Hardy entertains the Prince of Wales)

Lift latch, step in, be welcome, Sir,
Albeit to see you I'm unglad
And your face is fraught with a deathly shyness
Bleaching what pink it may have had,
Come in, come in, Your Royal Highness.

Beautiful weather?—Sir, that's true,
Though the farmers are casting rueful looks
At tilth's and pasture's dearth of spryness.—
Yes, Sir, I've written several books.—
A little more chicken, Your Royal Highness?

Lift latch, step out, your car is there,
To bear you hence from this antient vale.
We are both of us aged by our strange brief nighness,
But each of us lives to tell the tale.
Farewell, farewell, Your Royal Highness.

Max Beerbohm

LE MARCHAND D'AIL ET D'OIGNONS

A clove of garlic can keep
off the boredom of a call.
With onions cut small
an elegy's easy to weep.

Stéphane Mallarmé
Translated from the French by C. F. MacIntyre

U nless the talk be the finest "dish,"
No banquet's ever to my wish.

William Allingham

RADISHES

T hough pretty things, they like as not
Are either pithy or too hot,
Nor do you know, till you have bitten,
If you've a tiger or a kitten.

Richard Armour

LINES ON THE MERMAID TAVERN

Souls of Poets dead and gone,
What Elysium have ye known,
Happy field or mossy cavern,
Choicer than the Mermaid Tavern?
Have ye tippled drink more fine
Than mine host's Canary wine?
Or are fruits of Paradise
Sweeter than those dainty pies
Of venison? O generous food!
Dressed as though bold Robin Hood
Would, with his maid Marian,
Sup and browse from horn and can.

  I have heard that on a day
Mine host's sign-board flew away
Nobody knew whither, till
An Astrologer's old quill
To a sheepskin gave the story,—
Said he saw you in your glory,
Underneath a new-old sign
Sipping beverage divine,
And pledging with contented smack
The Mermaid in the Zodiac.

  Souls of Poets dead and gone,
What Elysium have ye known—
Happy field or mossy cavern—
Choicer than the Mermaid Tavern?

John Keats

HYMN TO THE BELLY

Room! room! make room for the bouncing Belly,
First father of sauce and deviser of jelly;
Prime master of arts and the giver of wit,
That found out the excellent engine, the spit,
The plow and the flail, the mill and the hopper,
The hutch and the boulter, the furnace and copper,
The oven, the bavin, the mawkin, the peel,
The hearth and the range, the dog and the wheel.
He, he first invented the hogshead and tun,
The gimlet and vise too, and taught 'em to run;
And since, with the funnel and hippocras bag,
He's made of himself that now he cries swag;
Which shows, though the pleasure be but of four inches,
Yet he is a weasel, the gullet that pinches
Of any delight, and not spares from his back
Whatever to make of the belly a sack.
Hail, hail, plump paunch! O the founder of taste,
For fresh meats or powdered, or pickle or paste!
Devourer of broiled, baked, roasted or sod!
And emptier of cups, be they even or odd!
All which have now made thee so wide i' the waist,
As scarce with no pudding thou art to be laced;
But eating and drinking until thou dost nod,
Thou break'st all thy girdles and break'st forth a god.

Ben Jonson

Table Talk

OH, FOR A BOWL OF FAT CANARY

Oh, for a bowl of fat Canary,
Rich Palermo, sparkling Sherry,
Some nectar else, from Juno's dairy;
Oh, these draughts would make us merry!

Oh, for a wench (I deal in faces,
And in other daintier things);
Tickled am I with her embraces,
Fine dancing in such fairy rings.

Oh, for a plump fat leg of mutton,
Veal, lamb, capon, pig, and coney;
None is happy but a glutton,
None an ass but who wants money.

Wines indeed and girls are good,
But brave victuals feast the blood;
For wenches, wine, and lusty cheer,
Jove would leap down to surfeit here.

John Lyly

WHAT WE EAT

There's often Weight in Things that seem the least,
And our most trifling Follies raise the Jest.

    The things we eat by various Juice control,
The Narrowness or Largeness of our Soul.
Onions will make even Heirs or Widows weep.
The tender Lettuce brings on softer Sleep.
Eat Beef or Pie-crust if you'd serious be:
Your Shell-fish raises *Venus* from the Sea:
For Nature that inclines to Ill or Good,
Still nourishes our Passions by our Food.

       William King

"TOUCH, CUP"

Touch, cup
      the lips
that drip
   honey
lick while you have them
I am not envious, but
wish that I had your luck.

       Leontios
    Translated from the Greek by Peter Jay

Table Talk

OYSTERS

Our shells clacked on the plates.
My tongue was a filling estuary,
My palate hung with starlight:
As I tasted the salty Pleiades
Orion dipped his foot into the water.

Alive and violated
They lay on their beds of ice:
Bivalves: the split bulb
And philandering sigh of ocean.
Millions of them ripped and shucked and scattered.

We had driven to that coast
Through flowers and limestone
And there we were, toasting friendship,
Laying down a perfect memory
In the cool of thatch and crockery.

Over the Alps, packed deep in hay and snow,
The Romans hauled their oysters south to Rome:
I saw damp panniers disgorge
The frond-lipped, brine-stung
Glut of privilege

And was angry that my trust could not repose
In the clear light, like poetry or freedom
Leaning in from sea. I ate the day
Deliberately, that its tang
Might quicken me all into verb, pure verb.

Seamus Heaney

Poems from the Table

SONG OF HATE FOR EELS

Oh, the slimy, squirmy, slithery eel!
He swallows your hook with malignant zeal,
He tangles your line and he gums your reel,
The slimy, squirmy, slithery eel.

Oh, the slimy, squirmy, slithery eel!
He cannot be held in a grip of steel,
And when he is dead he is hard to peel,
The slimy, squirmy, slithery eel.

Oh, the slimy, squirmy, slithery eel!
The sorriest catch in the angler's creel;
Who said he was fit for a Christian meal—
The slimy, squirmy, slithery eel!

Oh, the slimy, squirmy, slithery eel!
Malevolent serpent! who dares reveal
What eloquent fishermen say and feel
Concerning the slithery, slimy eel?

Arthur Guiterman

THE EEL

I don't mind eels
Except as meals.

Ogden Nash

SUSHI

"Why do we waste so much time in arguing?"
We were sitting at the sushi-bar
drinking *Kirin* Beer
and watching the Master chef
fastidiously shave
salmon, tuna and yellowtail
while a slightly more volatile
apprentice
fanned the rice,
every grain of which was magnetized
in one direction—east.
Then came translucent strips
of octopus,
squid and conger,
pickled ginger
and pale-green horseradish . . .
"It's as if you've some kind of death-wish.
You won't even talk . . ."
On the sidewalk
a woman in a leotard
with a real leopard
in tow.
For an instant I saw beyond the roe
of sea-urchins,
the erogenous
zones of shad and sea-bream;
I saw, when the steam
cleared, how this apprentice
had scrimshandered a rose's
exquisite petals

not from some precious metal
or wood or stone
("I might just as well be eating alone.")
but the tail-end of a carrot:
how when he submitted this work of art
to the Master—
Is it not the height of arrogance
to propose that God's no more arcane
than the smack of oregano,
orgone,
the inner organs
of beasts and fowls, the mines of Arigna,
the poems of Louis Aragon?—
it might have been alabaster
or jade
the Master so gravely weighed
from hand to hand
with the look of a man unlikely to confound
Duns Scotus, say, with Scotus Erigena.

Paul Muldoon

S aid Aristotle unto Plato,
    "Have another sweet potato?"
Said Plato unto Aristotle,
    "Thank you, I prefer the bottle."

Owen Wister

EATING SONG

(Being a Rendering of the Fervours of our best Drinking
Songs into the equivalent terms of a kindred Art)

If you want to drive wrinkles from belly and brow,
You must tighten the skin, as I tighten it now;
For at gobbets of bacon I sit at my ease,
And I button my mouth over dollops of cheese,
And I laugh at the Devil, who plays on his pipes
With the wind from a famishing traveller's tripes.
The French call it dining to peddle and peck,
But an Englishman's watchword is "Full to the neck!"
Does the parson deny it?—he's lean as a cat,
And the men that I like are all puffy and fat:
Perhaps you'll find music in heaven, but by George!
You won't get a thundering suetty gorge.
So down with your victuals, and stuff till you burst,
And let him who refuses a morsel be curst!

Sir Walter Raleigh

"FOR MY SOUL'S AND BODY'S FOOD"

For my soul's and body's food
I will take what does me good.
Spite of folk's or sages' cry,
Take what does me good will I.

William Allingham

ANY PART OF PIGGY

*A*ny part of piggy
Is quite all right with me
Ham from Westphalia, ham from Parma
Ham as lean as the Dalai Lama
Ham from Virginia, ham from York,
Trotters, sausages, hot roast pork.
Crackling crisp for my teeth to grind on
Bacon with or without the rind on
Though humanitarian
I'm not a vegetarian.
I'm neither crank nor prude nor prig
And though it may sound infra dig
Any part of darling pig
Is perfectly fine with me.

Noel Coward

"BERRIES, AND ALSO SEEDS"

*B*erries, and also seeds,
    Out of moments and moods they have sprung.
Pearls, or only glass beads,
    On a thread of life they are strung.

William Allingham

MENTAL DIGESTION

How strange, diverse, the powers of the mind!
E'en as the stomach can assimilate
And to itself subdue to affin'd state
Mere opposites of food and drink, divined
In bitter, sour, sweet; fish, flesh; coarse, refined,
Unerringly as needed; so create
Our minds from objects of our love and hate,
Their differences in degree and kind.
Poison to some, to others is as food;
Some will on garbage prey, tho' nectar were
At hand. One's evil is another's good.
From Dan unto Beersheba one will fare
And find all barren; while another would
In stones find sermons, and good everywhere!

Henry Ellison

VEGETARIANISM

These lower Lives eat Lives, I know;
A reason more *we* do not so,
Being Human, with a gleam and glow
Upon our life which travels far
From beyond the furthest star.
We know we are not as they are;
What they are, we do not know.

William Allingham

DRIED APPLE PIES

I loathe, abhor, detest, despise,
Abominate dried-apple pies.
I like good bread, I like good meat,
Or anything that's fit to eat;
But of all poor grub beneath the skies,
The poorest is dried apple pies.
Give me the toothache, or sore eyes,
But don't give me dried apple pies.
The farmer takes his gnarliest fruit,
'Tis wormy, bitter, and hard to boot;
He leaves the hulls to make us cough,
And don't take half the peeling off.
Then on a dirty cord 'tis strung
And in a garret window hung,
And there it serves as roost for flies,
Until it's made up into pies.
Tread on my corns, or tell me lies,
But don't pass me dried-apple pies.

Anonymous

Oh how I enjoy
Eating a ripe persimmon
While deep
Old bells boom!

Shiki
*Translated from the Japanese by Peter Beilenson
and Harry Behn*

Table Talk

LEMON PIE

The world is full of gladness,
 There are joys of many kinds,
There's a cure for every sadness,
 That each troubled mortal finds.
And my little cares grow lighter
 And I cease to fret and sigh,
And my eyes with joy grow brighter
 When she makes a lemon pie.

When the bronze is on the filling
 That's one mass of shining gold,
And its molten joy is spilling
 On the plate, my heart grows bold
And the kids and I in chorus
 Raise one glad exultant cry
And we cheer the treat before us—
 Which is mother's lemon pie.

Then the little troubles vanish,
 And the sorrows disappear,
Then we find the grit to banish
 All the cares that hovered near,
And we smack our lips in pleasure
 O'er a joy no coin can buy,
And we down the golden treasure
 Which is known as lemon pie.

Edgar A. Guest

MANNERS

Prig offered Pig the first chance at dessert,
So Pig reached out and speared the bigger part.

"Now that," cried Prig, "is extremely rude of you!"
Pig, with his mouth full, said, "Wha, wha' wou' 'ou do?"

"I would have taken the littler bit," said Prig.
"Stop kvetching, then it's what you've got," said Pig.

So virtue is its own reward, you see.
And that is all it's ever going to be.

Howard Nemerov

"GIVE ME ENOUGH OF MEAT AND DRINK"

Give me enough of meat and drink
That of meat and drink I may cease to think.
But what is enough? Much less, I trow,
Than all that ill habit longs for now.
And what is too little?—with all the rest,
My *whim* demands its share of the best.

William Allingham

Table Talk

SCIENCE AND GOOD-HUMOUR

A Feast of old was spread;
   The guests sat down, sings rumour,
With Science at their head,
   And at the foot Good-humour.
But soon, though rich the fare,
   One half the group sat pining,
While all the others there
   Were diligently dining.

🐝 🐝 🐝

On wines would Science chat,
   On alcohol and acid,
On vintage this and that,
   In accents slow and placid.
But while these maxims dropt,
   They set each listener thinking;
And there the wine had stopped,
   Had Humour not been drinking.

While Science, glass in hand,
   Show'd how 'twas manufactured;
Good-humour's jovial band
   A score of bottles fractured.
As Science proved, past doubt,
   That mirth we should not care for;
Good-humour laugh'd, without
   Inquiring why or wherefore.

Then rose a cry for song.
　　As Science led the table,
The call was loud and long
　　On vocalist so able.
But Science had—of course—
　　A cold, destroying music;
And fear'd that tones so hoarse
　　Would make both me and you sick.

His flourishings are vain,
　　Though each he twice rehearses;
To sing the song again,
　　He stops at fifteen verses.
Apollo has a hunch,
　　A gap is in the ballad;
No brandy's in the punch,
　　No lobster in the salad.

Good-humour now essays,
　　A careless, easy measure;
He sings, not he, for praise,
　　He only sings for pleasure.
His tones are not so clear,
　　And clouds the sparkles smother;
Yet though you stop one ear,
　　You open wide the other.

His slips in time and tune,
　　Had nigh set Science swearing;
But nightingales in June
　　Such censures might be sharing.

Table Talk

Right simple was the song,
    He sang it like a linnet;
'Twas not so very long,
    But something deep was in it.

Now forth at eventide
    They saunter,—some are rushing;
Through garden-walks they glide,
    A maze of blossoms blushing.
Here Science grew distressed,
    The flow'rs were not in order;
Good-humour liked them best
    When bursting through the border.

    ✻   ✻   ✻

As homeward now they stroll,
    The mind of Science stranded,
Good-humour feels his soul
    With rich delight expanded.
While Science, sleepy drone,
    His chamber seeks—the upper—
Good-humour, not alone,
    Is sitting down to supper.

Samuel Laman Blanchard

From THE CYNIC

Once at a merry wedding feast
A cynic chanced to be a guest;
Rich was the father of the bride
And hospitality his pride.
The guests were numerous and the board
With dainties plentifully stored.
There mutton, beef, and vermicelli,
Here venison stewed with currant jelly,
Here turkeys robbed of bones and lungs
Are crammed with oysters and with tongues.
There pickled lobsters, prawn, and salmon
And there a stuffed Virginia gammon.
Here custards, tarts, and apple pies
There syllabubs and jellies rise,
Ice creams, and ripe and candied fruits
With comfits and eryngo roots.
Now entered every hungry guest
And all prepared to taste the feast.
Our cynic cries—"How damned absurd
To take such pains to make a —!"

St. George Tucker

If things were better
   For me, flies,
   I'd invite you
To share my supper

Issa
*Translated from the Japanese by Peter Beilenson
and Harry Behn*

Table Talk

GREEN CORN

Wake, shake, day's a-breakin'
Peas in the pot and hoe-cakes a-bakin'.
Early in the morning, almost day;
If you don't come soon gonna throw it away.

Chorus:
Green corn, come along, Cholly,
Green corn, don't-cha tell Polly.
Green corn, come along Cholly.
Green corn, don't-cha tell Polly.
Green corn.

All I need in this creation,
Three months work and nine vacation.
Tell my boss any old time,
Daytime's his but nighttime's mine.

All I need to make me happy,
Two little kids to call me pappy.
One named Bill, the other Davy,
They like their biscuits slopped in gravy.

Anonymous

Poems from the Table

From FRUITS OF EXPERIENCE

Pomegranates come from red hot pearls.
Cherries are the hearts of baby girls.
Persimmons come up on the bosom of dawn.
Plums fill the sky when the day is gone.
Pineapples grow on the heads of kings.
Bananas are nothing but naughty things.

James Broughton

PICKLES

Since people are of many minds
About the sundry sorts and kinds,
Some way is needed to empower one
To tell a sweet one from a sour one.

Richard Armour

GRACE

Good bread,
  Good meat;
Good God!
  Let's eat!

Anonymous

Bacchus, Ceres
Pleaseth Venus

WHAT HARVEST HALF SO SWEET IS

What harvest half so sweet is
As still to reap the kisses
    Grown ripe in sowing?
And straight to be receiver
Of that which thou art giver,
    Rich in bestowing?
Kiss then, my Harvest Queen,
    Full garners heaping!
Kisses, ripest when th' are green,
    Want only reaping.

The dove alone expresses
Her fervency in kisses,
    Of all most loving:
A creature as offenseless
As those things that are senseless
    And void of moving.
Let us so love and kiss,
    Though all envy us:
That which kind, and harmless is,
    None can deny us.

Thomas Campion

CHERRY-RIPE

Cherry–Ripe! ripe! ripe! I cry,
Full and fair ones, come and buy:
If so be, you ask me where
They do grow? I answer, "There,
Where my Julia's lips do smile;
There's the land, or cherry isle,
Whose plantations fully show
All the year, where Cherries grow!"

Robert Herrick

From SONG

This peach is pink with such a pink
    As suits the peach divinely;
The cunning color rarely spread
    Fades to the yellow finely;
But where to spy the truest pink
Is in my Love's soft cheek, I think.

Norman Gale

PLUCK THE FRUIT
AND TASTE THE PLEASURE

$\mathcal{P}$ luck the fruit and taste the pleasure,
   Youthful Lordings, of delight;
Whilst occasion gives you seizure,
   Feed your fancies and your sight:
      After death, when you are gone,
      Joy and pleasure is there none.

Here on earth nothing is stable,
   Fortune's changes well are known;
Whilst as youth doth then enable,
   Let your seeds of joy be sown:
      After death, when you are gone,
      Joy and pleasure is there none.

Feast it freely with your lovers,
   Blithe and wanton sweets do fade,
Whilst that lovely Cupid hovers
   Round about this lovely shade:
      Sport it freely one to one,
      After death is pleasure none.

Now the pleasant spring allureth,
   And both place and time invites:
But, alas, what heart endureth
   To disclaim his sweet delights?
      After death, when you are gone,
      Joy and pleasure is there none.

Robert Lodge

Poems from the Table

"EVERY YEAR MEN HARVEST GRAPES"

Every year men harvest grapes, not seeing
    faded locks in severed tendrils.
But I reap love, and hold you, fruit of my
    devotion, in the gentle knot
of twining arms; nor could I reap elsewhere,
    so rich in charms are you. I wish
you young forever; yet, though wrinkles come
    like creepers, I will love you still.

            Macedonius
            Translated from the Greek by Adrian Wright

"WHENAS THE RYE REACH TO THE CHIN"

Whenas the rye reach to the chin
And chopcherry, chopcherry ripe within,
Strawberries swimming in the cream,
And school-boys playing in the stream;
    Then O, then O, then O my true love said,
        Till that time come again,
    She could not live a maid.

            George Peele

THE WORD *PLUM*

The word *plum* is delicious

pout and push, luxury of
self-love, and savoring murmur

full in the mouth and falling
like fruit

taut skin
pierced, bitten, provoked into
juice, and tart flesh

question
and reply, lip and tongue
of pleasure.

Helen Chasin

"FOR THE TASTE OF THE FRUIT"

For the taste of the fruit
is the tongue's dream,
& the apple's red
is the passion of the eye.

Erica Jong

LOVE'S HARVESTING

Nay, do not quarrel with the seasons, dear,
Nor make an enemy of friendly Time.
The fruit and foliage of the failing year
Rival the buds and blossoms of its prime.
Is not the harvest moon as round and bright
As that to which the nightingales did sing?
And thou, that call'st thyself my satellite,
Wilt seem in Autumn all thou art in Spring.
When steadfast sunshine follows fitful rain,
And gleams the sickle where once passed the plough,
Since tender green hath grown to mellow grain,
Love then will gather what it scattereth now,
And, like contented reaper, rest its head
Upon the sheaves itself hath harvested.

Alfred Austin

A BETROTHAL

Put your hand on my heart, say that you love me as
The woods upon the hills cleave to the hills' contours.

I will uphold you, trunk and shoot and flowering sheaf,
And I will hold you, roots and fruit and fallen leaf.

E. J. Scovell

Bacchus, Ceres Pleaseth Venus

AT THE GREEN CABARET 5 P.M.

For a full week, the soles of my boots had bled
On the cobblestones; I came to Charleroi.
At the Green Cabaret, I called for slices of bread
With butter, and ham which should not be too hot.

Quite happy, I stretched my legs beneath the table's
Green; I considered the artless histories
Of the tapestry. And it was wonderful, like the fables,
When the girl with the great breasts, she of the lively eyes,

—She's not the type that a kiss could frighten away!—
Laughing, she brought me bread and butter that lay
Upon a colored platter with ham half-cold,

Ham rosy and white, and perfumed with a dash
Of garlic, and she filled a great foaming glass
Which a ray of the tardy sun turned into gold.

Arthur Rimbaud
Translated from the French by Gerard Previn Meyer

THE EPICURE

(Sung by one in the Habit of a Town Gallant)

Let us drink and be merry, dance, joke, and rejoice,
With Claret and Sherry, Theorbo and Voice;
The changeable world to our joy is unjust,
All treasure uncertain, then down with your dust.
　　In frolic dispose your pounds, shillings and pence,
　　For we shall be nothing a hundred years hence.

We'll kiss and be free with Nan, Betty, and Philly,
Have oysters and lobsters, and maids by the belly;
Fish-dinners will make a lass spring like a flea,
Dame Venus (Love's goddess) was born of the sea.
　　With her and with Bacchus we'll tickle the sense,
　　For we shall be past it a hundred years hence.

Your most beautiful bit that hath all eyes upon her,
That her honesty sells for a hogo[1] of honour;
Whose lightness and brightness doth shine in such splendour
That none but the stars are thought fit to attend her,
　　Though now she be pleasant and sweet to the sense,
　　Will be damnably mouldy a hundred years hence.

Then why should we turmoil in cares and in fears,
Turn all our tranquillity to sighs and to tears?
Let's eat, drink and play till the worms do corrupt us,
'Tis certain that *post mortem nulla Voluptas.*[2]
　　Let's deal with our damsels, that we may from thence
　　Have broods to succeed us a hundred years hence . . .

Thomas Jordan

1. A taste or flavor　　2. After death there is no Pleasure.

ODE XII

They tell how Atys, wild with love,
Roams the mount and haunted grove;
Cybele's name he howls around,
The gloomy blast returns the sound!
Oft too by Claros' hallowed spring,
The votaries of the laurelled king
Quaff the inspiring magic stream,
And rave in wild prophetic dream.
But frenzied dreams are not for me,
Great Bacchus is my deity!
Full of mirth, and full of him,
While waves of perfume round me swim;
While flavored bowls are full supplied,
And you sit blushing by my side,
I will be mad and raving too—
Mad, my girl! with love for you!

Anacreon
Translated from the Greek by Thomas Moore

THE GOURMET'S LOVE-SONG

How strange is Love; I am not one
　　Who Cupid's power belittles,
For Cupid 'tis who makes me shun
　　My customary victuals.
Oh, EFFIE, since that painful scene
　　That left me broken-hearted,
My appetite, erstwhile so keen,
　　Has utterly departed.

My form, my friends, observe with pain,
　　Is growing daily thinner.
Love only occupies the brain
　　That once could think of dinner.
Around me myriad waiters flit,
　　With meat and drink to ply men;
Alone, disconsolate, I sit,
　　And feed on thoughts of Hymen.

The kindly waiters hear my groan,
　　They strive to charm with curry;
They tempt me with a devilled bone—
　　I beg them not to worry.
Soup, whitebait, entrées, fricassees,
　　They bring me uninvited.
I need them not, for what are these
　　To one whose life is blighted?

They show me dishes rich and rare,
    But ah! my pulse no joy stirs.
For savouries I've ceased to care,
    I hate the thought of oysters.
They bring me roast, they bring me boiled,
    But all in vain they woo me;
The waiters softly mutter, "Foiled!"
    The chef, poor man, looks gloomy.

P. G. Wodehouse

CAKES AND ALE

I gave her Cakes and I gave her Ale,
    I gave her Sack and Sherry;
I kissed her once and I kissed her twice,
    And we were wondrous merry.

I gave her Beads and Bracelets fine,
    I gave her Gold down derry.
I thought she was afeard till she stroked my Beard,
    And we were wondrous merry.

Merry my Hearts, merry my Cocks, merry my Sprights.
    Merry merry merry my hey down derry.
I kissed her once and I kissed her twice,
    And we were wondrous merry.

Anonymous

Poems from the Table

THE NURSE-LIFE WHEAT

The nurse-life wheat, within his green husk growing,
Flatters our hope and tickles our desire,
Nature's true riches in sweet beauties showing,
Which set all hearts with labor's love on fire.

No less fair is the wheat when golden ear
Shows unto hope the joys of near enjoying;
Fair and sweet is the bud, more sweet and fair
The rose, which proves that time is not destroying.

Caelica, your youth, the morning of delight,
Enameled o'er with beauties white and red,
All sense and thoughts did to belief invite,
That love and glory there are brought to bed;
    And your ripe years' love-noon—he goes no higher—
    Turns all the spirits of Man into desire.

Sir Fulke Greville

THE BRIDE-CAKE

This day my Julia thou must make
For Mistress Bride, the wedding cake:
Knead but the dough, and it will be
To paste of almonds turned by thee:
Or kiss it thou, but once, or twice,
And for the Bride-Cake there'll be spice.

Robert Herrick

ODE XLIX

When Bacchus, Jove's immortal boy,
The rosy harbinger of joy,
Who, with the sunshine of the bowl,
Thaws the winter of our soul;
When to my inmost core he glides,
And bathes it with his ruby tides,
A flow of joy, a lively heat,
Fires my brain, and wings my feet!
'Tis surely something sweet, I think,
Nay, something heavenly sweet, to drink!
Sing, sing of love, let Music's breath
Softly beguile our rapturous death,
While, my young Venus, thou and I
To the voluptuous cadence die!
Then waking from our languid trance,
Again we'll sport, again we'll dance.

Anacreon
Translated from the Greek by Thomas Moore

Poems from the Table

"THYRSIS AND MILLA, ARM IN ARM TOGETHER"

Thyrsis and Milla, arm in arm together,
In merry May to the green garden walked,
Where all the way they wanton riddles talked,
The youthful boy, kissing her cheeks all rosy,
Beseech'd her there to gather him a posy.

She straight her light green silken coats up tucked
And may for Mill and thyme for Thyrsis plucked,
Which when she brought he clasp'd her by the middle,
And kiss'd her sweet but could not read her riddle,
Ah fool, with that the Nymph set up a laughter,
And blush'd, and ran away, and he ran after.

Anonymous

"ABSTINENCE SOWS SAND ALL OVER"

Abstinence sows sand all over
The ruddy limbs and flaming hair,
But Desire Gratified
Plants fruits of life and beauty there.

William Blake

(ARTICHOKE, AFTER NERUDA)

It is green at the artichoke heart,
but remember the times
you flayed
leaf after leaf,
hoarding the pale silver paste
behind the fortresses of your teeth,
tonguing the vinaigrette,
only to find the husk of a worm
at the artichoke heart?
The palate reels like a wronged lover.
Was all that sweetness counterfeit?
Must you vomit back
world after vegetable world
for the sake of one worm
in the green garden of the heart?

Erica Jong

Poems from the Table

IN PRAISE OF COCOA,
CUPID'S NIGHTCAP

*Lines written upon hearing the startling
news that cocoa is in fact a mild aphrodisiac.*

Half past nine—high time for supper
"Cocoa love?" "of course my dear."
Helen thinks it quite delicious
John prefers it now to beer.
Knocking back the sepia potion,
Hubby winks, says, "Who's for bed?"
"Shan't be long," says Helen softly,
Cheeks a faintly flushing red.
For they've stumbled on the secret
of a love that never wanes
raft beneath the tumbled bedclothes,
cocoa coursing through their veins.

Stanley J. Sharpless

Sacred Fruit

Sacred Fruit

From THE GARDEN

What wondrous life is this I lead!
Ripe apples drop about my head;
The luscious clusters of the vine
Upon my mouth do crush their wine;
The nectarene, and curious peach,
Into my hands themselves do reach;
Stumbling on melons, as I pass,
Ensnared with flowers, I fall on grass.

Andrew Marvell

THE COUNTRY FAITH

Here in the country's heart
Where the grass is green,
Life is the same sweet life
As it e'er hath been.

Trust in a God still lives,
And the bell at morn
Floats with a thought of God
O'er the rising corn.

God comes down in the rain,
And the crop grows tall—
This is the country faith,
And the best of all!

Norman Gale

THE GRAIN OF MUSTARD SEED

Parable 7. Matthew 13

The grain of mustard seed is sown
Small, and despised: by means unknown,
It rises now, and branches throws,
In which the birds of heaven repose.

An emblem of the seed of grace!
At first, its progress scarce we trace,
Till, to prepare for flowers and fruits,
It spreads its limbs, and strikes its roots.

O, may our hearts this grace display,
Water'd, and growing, day be day!
May the immortal germ survive
Whate'er would harm, and in us thrive!

It must be planted here below,
And here its earliest buds must blow,
Still watch'd by heaven's unsleeping eye,
Or it will soon decline, and die!

Though now, of tenderest hue and form,
It shall withstand the roughest storm,
And bear, beyond this world of strife,
Its fruit to everlasting life!

Joseph Cottle

PRAISE OF CERES

With fair Ceres, Queen of Grain,
  The reapëd fields we roam, roam, roam:
Each country peasant, nymph, and swain,
  Sing their harvest home, home, home;
Whilst the Queen of Plenty hallows
Growing fields as well as fallows.

Echo, double all our lays,
  Make the champians sound, sound, sound
To the Queen of Harvest praise,
  That sows and reaps our ground, ground, ground.
Ceres, Queen of Plenty, hallows
Growing fields as well as fallows.

Thomas Heywood

LOGIC

Good wine maketh good blood,
Good blood causeth good humours,
Good humours cause good thoughts,
Good thoughts bring forth good works,
Good works carry a man to heaven;
Ergo, Good wine carrieth a man to heaven.

Anonymous

THE SEED SOWN

Parable 8. Matthew 13

Lord! the seed which thou dost sow,
Feed with dews, and let it grow!
May it bear, in young and old,
Fifty, and a hundred fold!

Let us not the seed display,
Lost and scatter'd by the way!
Never let it, Lord! be found
Wither'd on the stony ground!

Tares, too oft, obstruct the seed;
Now the thorn, and now the weed;
Cares, consuming, riches vain,
Choke the word, and prove its bane.

In our field, (our hearts of stone,)
Precious seed has oft been sown;
Harvest time is drawing near;
Where does now the fruit appear?

Let the seed which thou dost sow,
Take deep root, and upward grow;
And, unmoved by storm or blast,
Prove the tree of life, at last!

Joseph Cottle

Sacred Fruit

THREE OFFERINGS

Sosicles the farmer dedicated these sheaves
   from the furrows of his few acres to you
Demeter, friend of the wheat; his harvest was good.
   May later reapings also blunt his sickle.

A yellow-coated pomegranate, figs like lizards' necks,
   a handful of half-rosy part-ripe grapes,
a quince all delicate-downed and fragrant-fleeced,
   a walnut winking out from its green shell,
a cucumber with the bloom on it pouting from its leaf-bed,
   and a ripe gold-coated olive—dedicated
to Priapus friend of travellers, by Lamon the gardener,
   begging strength for his limbs and his trees.

Queen of black-earth Egypt, divine Isis
   in linen robes, accept my well-set offering:
flaky sacrificial cake on the wood-embers;
   two dazzling water-loving geese; nard
crumbled around seed-seething figs; raisins
   like lizard-skins; fragrant frankincense.
But most, great queen: save Damis from poverty
   as you did from the sea, and a gold-horned kid is yours.

Phillippos of Thessalonika
Translated from the Greek by Edwin Morgan

BREAD ENOUGH AND TO SPARE

The bread wherewith I have fed you in the wilderness.
—Exodus 16:32

Food of the soul, eternal bread,
    Which whoso eateth never dies;
Upon these desert sands spread out,
    The hidden manna of the skies.

True bread of heaven, and bread of God,
    In thee we find eternal store:
To thee in our deep need we come;
    Give us thyself for evermore.

True bread of life, the Father's gift,
    To feed the famished sons of earth;
Who eateth of thee hungers not,
    Even in this land of human dearth.

Life of the dead, O living Christ!
    Pour in Thy life into our death,
That we, all faint of soul, may know
    The power of Thine all-quickening breath.

Quickened by Thee, no death we fear;
    Sustained by Thee, our weakness turns
To strength immortal; touched by Thee,
    Our coldness into fervour burns.

Fed at Thy table, we are filled;
    Each day repeats the sweet repast,—
Sweeter and sweeter still, for Thou
    Keepest the best unto the last.

Horatius Bonar

From PARADISE LOST, *Book IX*

In the day we eate
Of this fair Fruit, our doom is, we shall die.
How dies the Serpent? hee hath eat'n and lives,
And knows, and speaks, and reasons, and discernes,
Irrational till then. For us alone
Was death invented? or to us deni'd
This intellectual food, for beasts reserv'd?
For Beasts it seems: yet that one Beast which first
Hath tasted, envies not, but brings with joy
The good befall'n him, Author unsuspect,
Friendly to man, farr from deceit or guile.
What fear I then, rather what know to feare
Under this ignorance of Good and Evil,
Of God or Death, of Law or Penaltie?
Here grows the Cure of all, this Fruit Divine,
Fair to the Eye, inviting to the Taste,
Of vertue to make wise: what hinders then
To reach, and feed at once both Bodie and Mind?
So saying, her rash hand in evil hour
Forth reaching to the Fruit, she pluckd, she eat:
Earth felt the wound, and Nature from her seat
Sighing through all her Works gave signs of woe,
That all was lost.

John Milton

From THE SUPPER OF THANKSGIVING

For the bread and for the wine,
For the pledge that seals Him mine,
For the words of love divine,
    We give Thee thanks, O Lord.

For the body and the blood,
For the more than angels' food,
For the boundless grace of God,
    We give Thee thanks, O Lord.

For the chalice whence we sip
Moisture for the parched lip,
For the board of fellowship,
    We give Thee thanks, O Lord.

For the feast of love and peace,
Bidding all our sorrows cease,
Earnest of the kingdom's bliss,
    We give Thee thanks, O Lord.

For the paschal lamb here given,
For the loaf without the leaven,
For the manna dropt from heaven,
    We give Thee thanks, O Lord.

Only bread and only wine,
Yet to faith the solemn sign
Of the heavenly and divine!
    We give Thee thanks, O Lord.

Horatius Bonar